HISTORY

OF THE

Pigeon Roost Massacre

BY

LIZZIE D. COLEMAN

COPYRIGHTED, 1904.

Commercial Print,
Mitchell, Indiana.

Official Directory of Scott County.

COUNTY OFFICERS.

Clerk	Noble J. Hays
Sheriff	Robert Peacock
Auditor	Frank Gardner
Treasurer	Alex Hough
Recorder	Jonathan F. Stark
Surveyor	M. N. Harbold
Coroner	Dr. J. B. Blocher, Jr.
Assessor	Joseph McClain
Superintendent of Public Schools	James A. Boatman
Com's : - 1st Dist	William Payne
2d Dist	Joseph Cortner
3d Dist	William L. Wilson

Commissioners' Court—First Monday in each month.

JUDICIAL OFFICERS.

Circuit Judge	Willard New
Prosecuting Attorney	Samuel B. Wells

COUNTY BOARD OF EDUCATION.

F. M. Hobbs	Finley
E. Chastine	Johnson
L. A. Davis	Jennings
P. F. Smith	Lexington
Asbury J. Thompson	Vienna

CITY OFFICERS OF SCOTTSBURG.

Clerk	H. G. Mitchell
Treasurer	Arthur Wyman
Attorney	Mark Storen
Marshal	George W. Walker
Trustees: 1st	John W. Allen
2d	Cecil C. Wells
3d	W. L. McClain

GOVERNOR WINFIELD T. DURBIN.

PIGEON ROOST MONUMENT, Near the Southwest corner of the Northwest fourth of the Northwest quarter of Section Seventeen, Town Two North, Range Seven East.

TO THE MONUMENT.

Oh men who died that autumn!
 And women and children, dear!
Who met thy fate in the wilderness
 When no kind friends were near;
Who suffered the sting of the arrow,
 And felt the hatchet's blow,
We raise to thee this monument,
 Our love and gratitude show.

By the side of the giant sassafras,
 Which marked those graves so long,
Which spread its branches over thee,
 And sang thee its lullaby song,
We raise thee this noble monument,
 That all who come may know
That the bodies of heroes and martyrs
 Lie buried far below.

Oh, sleep, sleep on, ye brave ones!
 For ye have earned thy rest,
Thy deeds have made thee honored,
 Thy sorrows have made thee blest;
For God who watches o'er us,
 Has recorded thy names on the roll;
Then sleep, sleep on, ye brave ones,
 Till heaven shall claim each soul.

                Lulu Dilley Donica.

PREFACE.

It is with a tinge of timidity that this little pamphlet is submitted to the public. Realizing that we have only vague accounts of this early defeat in our histories and they limited, we acknowledge that comparatively little is authentically known of the massacre.

Dillon's History, "Pigeon Roost Massacre," by Charles Martindale, "The Pigeon Roost Massacre," by John Mead, and an article from the Indianapolis News have been used as reference, but the greater part of the details were gathered from those now living in Scott and Washington Counties who were distantly related to the victims and have had their knowledge of the sad deed as a legacy from ancestry.

The part that the Paynes suffered in the sad event was obtained through the untiring efforts of Mrs. A. R. Overman, Salem, Indiana (grand-daughter of Jeremiah Payne), The details of the Collings' loss and geographical idea of the early settlement was gained from John and William Collings (grandson and great grandson of William E. Collings).

So in arranging, an earnest effort has been made to give the truth and tell the story as it really was.

In our feeble way a hearty thanks is here acknowledged to all who have so kindly assisted in gathering material and data.

> "Behind the scared squaw's birch canoe,
>   The steamer smokes and raves;
> And city lots are staked for sale
>   Above old Indian graves.
>
> "I hear the tread of pioneers
>   Of nations yet to be;
> The first low wash of waves,
>   Shall roll where soon a human sea."

PRELUDE.

A century ago Indiana Territory could have well been designated as Indian Territory; for living in their savage wigwam on all the frontiers was that red-skin, which was a menace to universal peace. The Indian, at his best, does not present a very facinating appearance; nevertheless with a tall, strong body resembling in color old copper; with hair like a horse's mane, coarse, black and straight; with small eyes, black and deep-set; with high cheek bones and a prominent nose, dabbed permiscuously with paint, together with the crudeness and barbarity of dress, he is a personage of interest. But this outward appearance is as naught in revealing the individuality of the tribe. When at peace they are hospitable and friendly; when in war they are merciless and brutal. When conquering, if they failed to make their victim cry out with pain they considered it an ill omen; therefore they would tear out bits of flesh, roast their victim in a slow fire while they continued to sing his death-song, with an unwavering voice, until his last breath released him from their torments.

At this time, dotted here and there in the various territories were the respective Indian tribes. Each locality having a certain class, while our territory was the only one that was not permanent headquarters for certain tribes. Yet out soil furnished a meeting place for members of different tribes during the various depredations. And as navigation was the only means of transportation during those times we can readily see why certain places were selected as "hunting grounds" and temporary abodes.

Nevertheless along all our frontiers were the forts (or block-houses) the one needed, lasting characteristic of those early days. Generally some central place in each settlement would be selected for the building of the fort. Besides locality the supply of water must be considered, for without this in time of trouble the inmates would famish. The fort furnished a home for the defenseless and a place of refuge from the hand of the savage. These forts (or block-houses) were constructed of round logs and usually were two stories high. The logs used in the upper story were four feet longer than those below, thus providing an aperture through which to use their rifles. In the upper story were portholes large enough to shoot balls from rifles, striking the ground at an angle. All around the fortification, timbers nine feet high were stuck in the ground and thus was formed an inclosure for all that they wished to defend from a savage invasion.

But mindful of all this, the one undefended settlement in all the territory furnished the stage for performing the last mas-

8

sacre in the Northwest Territory. This section of land, many years prior to its sad fate, was thickly covered with timber and became a favorite rendezvous for passenger or wild pigeons. The number was so great that trees were twisted, bent and broken by the great weight upon them and thousands of pigeons were annually killed by falling timber. Separated from all others by an intervening distance of five or six miles was this one fertile spot in the midst of surrounding sterility—the one place that was habitable for man and the one eyed because of its productiveness, for the abundance of game was quite an item in maintaining a livelihood for a family.

Thus, when our early fathers cleared the land here in 1809, they gave the memorable name of "Pigeon Roost" to the settlement and to the beautiful stream near. While settling, and for two years, the hardships, privations and perils were equally enjoyed and shared by the white man with his predecessor, the Indian.

Enjoying as we do all the advantages and appliances of modern civilization, it is almost impossible for us to realize how these early settlers lived—no complete government, crude homes and no conveniences for living or working, no division of labor so that the accomplishment of any one thing was hardly realized. Each family busy in supplying their meager demands. Log houses, consisting of but one room, occupied by an entire family were theirs; scant furniture with a poor variety of food, mostly meal and game, were adjuncts to their welfare, yet they were industrious and thrifty as far as they were able.

North of the "Pigeon Roost" settlement lived Jeremiah and Elias Payne (brothers), Isaac Coffman and Dan Johnson with their wives and children. The wives of Elias Payne, Coffman and Johnson were sisters and their maiden name was Bridgewater. So these in their relations were as one—one interest and a life in common.

The families that composed these early settlements were related and having built their houses near each other it was almost as one big family. A quarter of a mile southeast from the now imposing shaft that marks the hallowed resting place of its early inhabitants lived the venerable William E. Collings. At home with him, enjoying the blessings of the parental roof, were the two youngest children, Lydia and John. Several children were grown and had homes of their own. A hundred yards east from the old home of father was the humble home of Henry Collings. Three-quarters of a mile east was the crude log-house that sheltered Richard Collings and his wife, with their seven children. West and south were two sons and two daughters. Jane Collings Biggs (wife of John Biggs) and Sichey Collings Richie (wife of Dr. John Richie) with their children were in the im-

9

mediate settlement. Other residents of this early colony made the entire population not more than thirty-five.

We are cognizant of the Indian's love for the rifle and his ability as a marksman. In these pioneer days the "shooting matches" were the one great sport and the phenomenal ability of William E. Collings was sorely realized by them. In fact he was such a champion that "Long Knife" was the name the Indians gave him, and soon the names of all the participants were readily exchanged in combating. One day after a friendly "shooting match" the Indians told "Long Knife" that they were going away. Mr. Collings kindly asked them to come back some day and told them that he would give them the best he had (we would infer that he meant that he would share his hospitality and be a combatant in a champion game). So they departed and these early pioneers were alone—the quietness of the Indian nature was no more.

During the summer of 1812 along many of our frontiers, starvation stared the Indians in the face and their "hunting grounds" were becoming inadequate for their demands. Little insignificant incidents were growing almost as mountains to this vicious race. They held green in memory their losses at the recent battle of Tippecanoe. They imagined that they were being cheated in all their trades; were being spied and encroached upon while seeking their wonted haunts, and they well knew of the reward offered by the British Government for the scalp of every American white. So that part of their nature which had been dormant for some time had kindled a spark and they were plotting revenge.

The crowning act to cause the Indians to actively show this spirit was stimulated by the disgraceful surrender of Hull at Detroit, less than a month before the shameful attack upon the innocent dwellers of "Pigeon Roost." The news of this surrender filled the hearts of all with a feeling of indescribable horror for the anticipated actions of the Indians might be realized in the beastly use of tomahawk and scalping knife.

The possibilities of attack were soon realized—simultaneously among many of these settlements were the bands of savage redskins armed with implements that meant death and fired with a beastly nature for revenge.

But of all the settlements the one at "Pigeon Roost" was the one to be pitied. In their simple, easy way they had lived in common with the Indian, shared his hardships, enjoyed his sports, and the thought of needing a place of defense—of safety, had never been realized.

Prior to the massacre, Shawnee and Pottawatomie Indians had a camp west of the present site of Vienna (one mile and a half northeast from monument). Here doubtless they recounted their ill feelings, multiplied their grievances and planned to appease

10

their thirst for blood. Many of them knew of the advantages of "Pigeon Roost," its unparalleled location, fertility of soil and abundance of game, thus making an ideal hunting ground, also of its defenseless condition. And so in the story that follows, we may sadly trace the savage, brutal and beastly nature of the enemy of the early "Pigeon Roost" settlers.

"They knew of their enemy,
But, ah then they had no time to prepare for them.
And many and many fell by the foe,
Because they had no place to go."

STORY OF THE MASSACRE.

From the early settlers of Scott County we learn that they were personally told by Mr. Sparks how the Indians crossed White River at Sparksville, Indiana, September 3, 1812, on a southern mission. They crossed the river three or four at a time; after all had crossed they formed together and directed their way to the ill-fated spot now hallowed in memory to the early victims.

During the afternoon they had reached the field of action and simultaneously several homes were visited.

Jeremiah Payne (who lived near a fort at Vienna, but seven miles north from Pigeon Roost) was warned of danger when his cows, bellowing very loud, came running to the house with spears and arrows stuck in their sides. Taking his wife and only child, Lewis, to the fort at Vienna, the father started on foot to warn his only brother, Elias (who lived five miles away), of their threatened trouble. He ran in a "turkey trot" as he called it— but too late. He found that the Indians had been before him and already done their deadly work. The wife and seven children of his brother had been massacred—part of their bodies cut into strips and strung around trees, parts put in the house and after plundering the home, they took the feather beds, tore them open so the feathers were scattered over everything, then set the house on fire. "Old Uncle Jerry" said that he thus saw a smoke that was as black as ink, and there was a stench that was terrible. One authority says that one more skeleton was found among these remains than comprised the famliy, so it is a mere matter of conjecture that accidentally an Indian was also burned. In the meantime Elias Payne and his brother-in-law, Isaac Coffman, were in the woods, two miles north of "Pigeon Roost" hunting "bee trees." While thus engaged, a band of Indians, ten or twelve in number unexpectedly fired upon them. Coffman was instantly killed and scalped. His bleached bones were found afterwards

11

1

2

3

4

5

6

with the buckets of honey near. Payne, accompanied by his dog, was pursued two miles before overtaken and mortally wounded. The story is told that his dog went back to known places and after several trips to the fatal spot led his master's brother, Jeremiah, to the fatal beech tree where the dying brother was found. A bed of flax was made and the mangled victim was here laid while the over-anxious brother went for help. On his return the life spark had gone out and the sad victim had never been able to speak or recognize his brother. The body was buried on the spot and the place is to-day discernible, being on the Salem road due west from Vienna.

Thus the passiveness became active and the frenzied group wend their way to the south.

Another unprotected woman, Mrs. Richard Collings, and her seven children (Mr. Collings being away in the service of the government), are soon in the thralldom of the savage mob in their own home. Their lives are soon taken, bodies left in the one loved spot on earth and all offered as a precious sacrifice to appease the red-skin's bloody thirst. A foot log across Pigeon Roost Creek marks the spot where these ashes and bones were found.

When we remember that they were so perfected in the art of scalping that a body could be disposed of in one minute, we can faintly see how quick they were ready for more human material.

Going southwest from here, they met Mrs. Rachael Collings (wife of Henry) who had just returned home from Payne's where she had been to get spools for warping. Words are inadequate for describing the barbarity of results here. Mrs. Collings was pregnant at the time, having been made the victim of the Indian mob, the child was taken from the womb and scalped, afterwards found laid on the bosom of the woman. The incentive to such a diabolical deed was the five-dollar British reward offered for each scalp.

Having nerved themselves to anything, they approach more familiar spots in the well-known home of their brave competitor, William E. Collings, not having in their mind the friendliness that existed when they left a few months before, not with a response to a friendly "shooting match' but fired with a vengeance

---

NOTE, referring to pictures on page 12: 1, Jeremiah Payne's house near Harristown. 2, John W. Martin, Trustee of Monument. 3, Sarah Payne, daughter of Jeremiah Payne; born January 12, 1818, in Clark county; married Asbury Garriott; died January 31, 1901. 4, Mary Payne, daughter of Jeremiah Payne; married Jacob Day. 5, W. T. Hubbard, Scottsburg, contractor for purchase and erection of monument. 6. Apple tree planted by Jeremiah Payne, still living and bearing fruit.

that meant ultimate devastation, destruction and death, and that in the worst form imaginable.

In this Collings home on this memorable afternoon was the aged father, Lydia and Captain Norris, an old Indian fighter, who had engaged in the battle of Tippecanoe and was here now to warn the settlers of their threatened danger. This distinguished guest was a native of Pennsylvania, and realizing what the impending possibilities were to the settlers of "Pigeon Roost" had come to confer with them concerning the need of a fort.

The Captain and Collings had been talking but a short time, perhaps not more than an hour. While William E. Collings was saying that he felt as safe as if he was in Philadelphia, Captain Norris espied the Indians approaching. Collings said that they would go into the cabin and fight until they died. Whereupon Collings grasped a gun and handed one to Captain Norris, but he could not handle it easily, having been severely wounded in the shoulder in the recent battle of Tippecanoe. Norris strongly argues that it would be the valiant part for him and his children to attempt to escape but they cannot because of being seen, and they know that with the darkness their lives—their all, will be in danger in the house.

So they plan to try and defend themselves until dark and then attempt flight. Thus the father, a man sixty years of age, nerving himself for the arduous duties before him, justly earns the name of "Long Knife" while Lydia moulds the bullets. We remember that Henry's house is just a hundred yards away; the Indians are plundering the house while the anxious ones in the old homestead are watching every movement. While thus busily engaged, William E. Collings, espying a big Indian standing in the doorway (at Henry's) steals up behind him, takes good aim, fires, and the force of the murdering foe is reduced. Of course this loss stirs up the already heat of the Indian band and they are almost desperate in making strokes count around their old rival's home. One Indian assumes the appearance of a woman, having decked himself in Mrs. Henry Collings' shawl, and while thus plotting he falls a victim at the hand of the matchless marksman.

In the meantime John, aged thirteen, had caught a horse and was ready to go after the cows when he saw an Indian approaching. Dropping the rein he fled, but was pursued. He realized that the savage was gaining on him when he heard the report of his father's rifle, followed by a "boo;" glancing back he saw the savage fall with the blood streaming from his breast. Now he knew that he was saved and quickly made his way to the house.

For three-quarters of an hour the old home was defended and the occupants were safe, while four Indians had fallen. Thus a good cause for the Indians to need to hold counsel. While they

14

were thus engaged under cover of night, the family made their
way from the house to the corn field near. They knew enough of
the Indian nature that with the darkness their house would be
fired and they would probably be burned alive. Lydia went first,
then John, followed by Captain Norris, and lastly by the dear,
brave old hero, William E. Collings. As the latter passed the
corn crib an Indian who was lurking behind it fired. Collings
raised his gun to return the shot when he found that the savage
in missing his aim had broken the lock of his wonderful gun.
He halloed to Norris to "send back his gun until I kill this raid
of s— of ———." But Norris, like the Irishman, "had a brave
heart, but a cowardly pair of legs," and Collings was alone to
meet the enemy. When they came too near he would raise his
flintlock and pretend that he would fire and thus frighten them.
They knew by the many successful "shooting matches" they had
had that he was more than their equal and that a bullet from his
gun meant death. So for Collings, the useless gun was his sal-
vation; had he fired the Indian would have known what direction
he took and he would have been the victim of bullet or tomahawk

WILLIAM C. COLLINGS.
Present owner of the Cap Gun used in the Massacre.

and later the scalping knife. Thus he made his way through the
corn, came near John Richie's (son-in-law), fell down a tree,
and the Indians were so near that he could see the white of their
eye, but eventually he made his escape and early next morning
was sheltered in the fort at his son, Zebulon's, five miles south
from "Pigeon Roost" settlement.

15

Meanwhile Captain Norris and the children were repeatedly lost; tired from their journey they sat down at the foot of a big oak and fell asleep. Captain Norris said that he never slept more sound in all his life, yet with the rising sun they were on their march and made their way in safety to the blockhouse.

Henry Collings, who was at work in the field, was wounded in the head by an unexpected missile. He cautiously made his way to an old shed and concealed himself under a pile of flax. Here he was found a day or two later more dead than alive. He rallied and in a whisper faintly said: "I went to jump the fence and 'Little Kill Buck' shot me." Such recognition proves that these early martyrs knew who their murderers were.

Others massacred were the mother, wife and only child of John Morris. Can we imagine the anguish of this man's heart when returning home from government service to find his loss threefold, his all, gone?

During the hour that the Indians were busy scalping their victims, plundering the homes and burning the houses, several were making their escape.

About sundown Mrs. Jane Collings Biggs, followed by two children and carrying a baby in her arms, went into the woods to look for her cow. On her return, reaching the edge of the clearing, she was horrified to hear the repeated yells of a band of Indians who had surrounded her home. Understanding what it meant she turned and started through the forest to her brother's six miles away. Occasionally she would look back; once while scanning she was awe stricken to see her home in flames and hear the march of hurried feet and loud voices. In fact the foe had gained and was just a hundred yards away. What must she do? At this critical moment the baby began crying and the poor mother hastily stuffed a corner of her woolen shawl into its mouth. Baby-like it repulsed this and noise issued. Suddenly the Indians stopped as if they had heard a sound. Can we for a moment imagine how long time must have been to this over-burdened, over-anxious, helpless mother? One minute was an eternity while the Indians passed out of sight. When she withdrew her hand the child was silent, was motionless, yea dead. In her fear and anxiety for their safety she had smothered her darling. Poor mother! She sank to the ground overcome with grief, but presently she rallied and slowly continued her march to her brother's. About daylight, with her dead baby in her arms and the two little ones holding at her skirt she was safe. How long the way must have been, how lonesome the steps, how heavy the heart burden.

"A mother with her babies three
Had gone to the field for her cow, you see;

16

She heard the shriek of the angry foe
And tried to make her escape, you know.

The infant in the mother's arms,
She thought was making some alarm;
She stuffed its mouth with her woolen shawl,
In order to stop its little squall.

She looked around, her house in flames;
"What can I do? Oh God," she screams,
"Five miles is the closest place I know,
To shelter my babies from the foe."

The enemy's shriek was heard again,
On they passed without seeing them;
The mother clasped her babies in her arms,
And thanked God that they were unharmed.

On to her brother's house she went,
For as we learned her house was burned;
But sad it was to that dear mother's eyes,
When she found she had killed her babe
      to smother its cries."

Dr. John Richie (son-in-law of William E. Collings) was at work in the field; espying the enemy he hastened home and told his wife Sichey. Taking her upon his back he went through the cornfields to the woods, where quietly and cautiously they waited for the dawn. When they dared risk traveling they left their hiding place and sought refuge at the fort.

Mrs. Betsy Johnson, sister of Mrs. Elias Payne, also reached the fort without being molested. During the afternoon she heard the screams of children and justly realizing the cause left her home. While on the journey she looked back and saw her house in flames.

Ben Yount, hearing the shooting of guns and comprehending the danger, put his wife on a horse behind him, took his children in their arms and went to the fort at Silver Creek (eight miles south of Vienna). That night they were the proud but anxious parents of another daughter, Rachel. This child in after years became the wife of William Cravens, step-mother to William and Nelson Cravens, Scottsburg.

We must remember that many of the men were away in the service of the government, so the women and children were seemingly helpless. The Indians knew of their great advantage and in making their ravages they planned well their line of march.

A Mrs. Beal, who lived in or near the settlement and whose

husband was with Captain Pitman at Vincennes, heard the frenzied Indians. Taking her two little ones, she went to a sink-hole for protection. Here she remained until eight or nine o'clock at night, when she made her way to the fort, arriving at two o'clock in the morning.

Each tragic event of history carries with it many phases, many different means of protection. Of the Norris family it is said that the father, Edward, wanted to take his family to the fort, but the wife insisted on staying at home and trust in God to take care of them. They had a very small piece of land cleared, had two horses, two cows and two hounds. During the night the cows ran around the house and bellowed, the hounds barked and howled while the inmates of the humble cabin smelt blood. Nevertheless the mother was up all night and carded wool, also spun the rolls into yarn to make clothes for her family.

Many in abandoning their homes turned over stands of bees to bother the frenzied intruders. The brave pioneers had perilous experiences. The hours of this afternoon and night were as a life-time.. While several escaped they knew little compared with butchering and roasting of those within the hand of the savage foe.

And so within one hour the settlement was in a deplorable condition. Those who had espied the fatal enemy or heard the cry of children, were on their way to the fort fearful of any unforeseen occurence, while their comrades who had been overtaken without a moment's notice, were in the murderer's hands and in the thralldom of the red-skin. Their work of one hour meant the loss of twenty-two lives. The Indians were gone. The massacre was over.

SEQUEL.

Jeremiah Payne having taken his wife and son to the fort, and realizing the terrible condition of the helpless ones in the settlement, mounts his fast horse and starts to New Albany for help. At dusk he was on his way. The road was through the woods, unfortunately he took the wrong way, causing such delay that he did not reach his destination until early daylight. He, with a company of mounted riflemen, started for the settlement. Along the road they were joined by many more until their force numbered two or three hundred. They arrived at the ill-fated spot about two o'clock the afternoon of the fourth. Judge Isaac Naylor, an eye witness thus describes: "Oh, what a mournful scene met our vision as we beheld the log cabins and the mangled bodies of men and women and children, their once happy inmates. I had seen the Tippecanoe battle-fields strewn with dead

18

and dying soldiers; they had fallen in deadly strife with a savage foe whom they had conquered; they had fallen in a soldier's costume, a soldier's armor and were entitled to a soldier's grave. Not so in Pigeon Roost Massacre; here all were doomed to indiscriminate slaughter, from the suckling babe to the hoary-headed grandmother and grandsire. Neither age, nor sex, nor beauty, nor innocence could stay the hand of the merciless savage."

About three o'clock this same afternoon (September 4th) the trail of the enemy was found and the company under the command of Major John McCoy tracked the murderers for several miles. They were at the banks of the Muscatatuck, which was so swollen that they could not cross. Darkness was upon them and nothing effectual could be accomplished and they were compelled to encamp.

The morning of the fifth these who were bent on revenge but who had been repulsed (the Indians having several hours advance on their march) returned to the sad scene of action, collected the partial remains of the charred and cut bodies and buried them.

On the sixth the militia were reinforced by sixty mounted volunteers under the command of Captain McFarland from Jefferson County. On the afternoon of the seventh, three hundred and fifty volunteers from Kentucky were on the field ready to assist the Indiana companies in avenging the wrong. Attempts were made towards military organization, but rivalry between officers whose sole ambition was to command the troops, caused it to fail. All returned to their homes cherishing with sadness the fate of their early neighbors, fired with a zeal to sometime avenge the wrong and realizing the power of the Indian when in his frenzied mood.

The settlement was again inhabited. William E. Collings could be found in his old home, that with its bullet holes told the story of the massacre and the heroic defense. While the other families were compelled to build new cabins. So for years the Collings lived in Pigeon Roost. The children to the third and forth generation treasuring with fondest memory the one unharmed home of the fatal fall day and all that spoke of the struggle. Yea, to-day it is an oasis in their experience to again live over those experiences for it is sympathy of blood for blood.

But it was with a great degree of alarm and sudden fear of danger that kept the entire settlement in a constant unsatisfied condition.

Zebulon Collings (son of William E. Collings) thus describes their grave situation: "The manner in which I used to work in those perilous times was as follows: On all occasions I carried my rifle, tomahawk and butcher-knife in my belt. When I went to plow I laid my gun on the plowed ground and stuck up a stick

19

by it for a mark so that I could get it quick in case it was wanted. I had two good dogs; I took one into the house leaving the other out. The one outside was expected to give the alarm which would cause the other inside to bark, by which I would be awakened, having my arms always loaded. I left my horses in the stable close to the house, having a port-hole so that I could shoot to the stable door. During two years I never went from home with any certainty of returning, not knowing the minute I might receive a ball from an unknown hand; but in the midst of all these dangers that God, who never sleeps nor slumbers, has kept me."

After 1815 these pioneers were not disturbed by invasions and murderous slaughters, yet many prior to this time had an eye ever ready to avenge the fiendish savage.

Various accounts are given of the actions and marches of the Indians, who were the participants in the cruel massacre.

They were gone by sunrise the morning of the fourth day after their cruel deed going north anticipatingly to their temporary camp. They attempted to cross the river at Sparksville on this return home but the white man was prepared for them and anxiously waited, desiring to rid themselves of the red-skin's terror.

When they came to the river they were loaded with trophies of their victory—quilts, bedding, etc. As they went into the river white men watched their chances. The water was shallow on the north side—they went in on that side and when the Indians would get about half way across the river the white men would fire. Repeatedly they were repulsed, so they went west and crossed the river at Shoals. Mr. Sparks sat in the corner of his garden and fired. He showed Mr. William Cravens where this attempt at crossing was made.

Having crossed the river they were soon at their camp on the Kankakee River on a reservation between Kankakee and Lake Counties, at which place they feel safe, being completely surrounded by water; the river here is so perfectly level.

When settled in camp they enjoyed a war dance. Can the barbarity of such a time be imagined, when they would dance, riot and yell in thinking of the scalps they had taken and prospectively of their financial gain? Not only the quantity was great in their eyes but the hideousness, brutality and heartlessness of the manner in which they had worked in winning their treasure seemed to put their being on fire.

Besides they had something else with them that added to their festivity and dance. Somehow they had managed while on their Pigeon Roost trip to steal a little girl that made her home with Jeremiah Payne. She was the child of an uncle of Mrs. Jeremiah Payne. Although but three years old at this sad time,

20

through her varied perils and experiences she remembered her true name, Ginsey McCoy (see further account in Supplement).

After rioting, some of the Indians scattered to their respective headquarters, the Shawnee to their chief on the Tippecanoe and the Pottawatomie to their camps near the present site of Chicago. Other depredations and attacks were made in various places in our territory during the next two years.

In 1815 the Pottawatomie Indians were on another southern invasion but they were able to go no further south than Leesville, Lawrence County. Here within a few hundred yards of the little village an old man named Flinn was killed, a young man Flinn (son of other Flinn) was captured and his son-in-law, Guthrie, wounded. Thus the feeling of unrest because of this roar in our territory was over.

Having followed the Indians, the work of pursuit and the inhabiting of the settlement, we want to go back to the sad scene of burying the dead on the memorable days following the massacre. Seventeen bodies were killed outright, others were left in a mangled, dying condition, which eventually increased the number of deaths to twenty-two—twenty-two sacrificed to appease the nature of the merciless Indian.

Many bodies were so badly disfigured as not to be recognizable, so cut and so charred, part of their bodies had been pierced by sticks and stuck in trees and then fired. While with others bones and ashes were the only remains. These fragments were with difficulty collected and placed in three graves, side by side (sixteen in one grave and the remaining six in two other graves) on a hillside a quarter of a mile northwest from the home of the brave defender, William E. Collings.

A few rough stones have during these many years marked the sacred spot and a mammoth sassafras, nature's mark for this historic hollowed place, has stood as a sentinel over their sacred dust. Somehow nature's law has been almost phenomenal in thus spanning the size and lengthy endurance of nature's monument. A tree that measures now fourteen feet in girth at the ground and has, with its large, shining leaves, fed no doubt, by the mould from the sleeping dead, been a constant reminder of pioneer bravery. How sweet the thought, how pleasant the idea that God fittingly marked this place as a memorial, a marker, a monument that towers higher than a tree, larger at the base and strong enough to bear the changes for ages. The giant old sassafras was to this spot what the spring was to the inmates of Libby Prison, the life-spring held before each an example of fortitude, and left such an impression on the friends that agitation for a lasting marker passed from a possibility to a glorious reality.

21

PANORAMIC VIEW OF THE MONUMENT:

"Yes, forgotten by some,
By others yet unknown,
But instead of a tree,
Is erected a mark of stone."

Through the efforts of James W. Fortner, Jeffersonville, Indiana, at the sixty-third General Assembly of Indiana on February 11, 1903, the following was approved:

"Whereas, the tomb of the pioneer heroes massacred at Pigeon Roost is without a monument, therefore

Section 1. Be it enacted by the General Assembly of the State of Indiana that there be hereby appropriated out of any funds in the State Treasury not otherwise appropriated the sum of two thousand dollars for the purpose of purchasing and erecting a monument over the graves of the said pioneer heroes."

James W. Fortner, President, John W. Martin, Secretary, and Joseph H. Hodapp, Treasurer, were the trustees appointed to contract for purchase and erection of the monument.

To-day, side by side with the giant old sassafras, which is nearing the end of its existence and already shows many signs of decay, is the imposing monument of stone. Occupying as it does a prominent place on this historic hillside with a height of forty-two feet, it speaks of pioneer fortitude and modern acknowledgment of such.

The shaft is of Indiana origin, being taken from the Indiana Bedford Stone Company at Oolitic, Lawrence County. It was

22

shaped and dressed in the monumental shop of John A. Rowe, Bedford, Indiana. The contractor for the purchase and erection of the monument was W. T. Hubbard, Scottsburg, Indiana. The

VIEWS OF MONUMENT IN COURSE OF ERECTION.

monument was raised October 27, 1903, during the succeeding weeks the lettering and polishing were finished. The monument is in four parts; (1) B base, 10 feet by 10 feet by 1 foot 9 inches;

(2) 2a base, 7 feet 3 inches by 1 foot 6 inches by 1 foot 6 inches ;
(3) die, 5 feet 4 inches by 5 feet 4 inches by 5 feet 6 inches ;
(4) spire, (base) 2 feet 10 inches by 2 feet 10 inches by 34 feet ;

THE MONUMENT IN PLACE.

(top) 1 foot 11 inches by 1 foot 11 inches.

The inscriptions are:

(1) The Sixty-third General Assembly of Indiana appropriated $2,000.00 for the erection of this monument. Approved February 11, 1903, by Winfield T. Durbin, Governor of Indiana.

24

(2)   In memory of the Pioneer Heroes,
              Twenty-two in Number,
   Massacred at Pigeon Roost Defeat by the Shawnee Indians.
                 September 3, 1812.
(3)   Trustees, James W. Fortner, President.
              John W. Martin, Secretary.
              Joseph W. Hodapp, Treasurer.
              W. T. Hubbard, Contractor.

(4) The fourth side has a large bronze plate with a fac simile of the sad scene during the massacre.

With the fall days again upon us our minds return to the sad story of the massacre and with these thoughts in mind the final step is taken. October 1, 1904, the monument is formally dedicated as a permanent memorial to the pioneer heroes.

SUPPLEMENT TO THE STORY.

Interesting little stories come from various sources as links by which we see how the Indians were feeding their nature preparatory for trouble.

(1) A number of Indians were staying over night with Dan Johnson. They had with them a white elk which they left in the stable for safe keeping. The next morning it could not be found and the luckless Johnson was accused of being cognizant of its disposal.   MEAD.

(2) An Indian and white man were engaged in a horse trade. The after thought of the Indian was that he had been shamefully cheated. The next day he went back to the white man to call it all off but this was refused. Naturally his angry passions were grievously taxes.   MEAD.

(3) The story goes that Collings had sold a quantity of whiskey to a band of Indians. While they were under the influence of this Collings bought some furs from the Indians. They imagined that they were the great losers and had been terribly cheated. In their revengeful way they attempted to burn and destroy. This happened during the hunting season before the massacre.
                        CRAVENS

SUMMARY OF DEATHS.
September 3, 1812.

Henry Collings.
Rachael Collings (wife of Henry).
Mrs. Richard Collings and seven children.
Mrs. John Morris and child.
Mrs. Morris (mother of John Morris).
Mrs. Elias Payne.
Mr. Elias Payne and seven children

25

The one relic of this massacre is the flintlock gun used by William E. Collings during his brave defense. Its record at this time is the successful killing of four Indians in four successive shots. The fifth attempt it was found that the main spring had been broken.

Before the decease of the dear old father he willed this heirloom to his son, John, but he thought it of no value and it became the property of his brother, Karnes. Here it remained for some time, but before his death, at public sale, this broken, useless treasure became the property of his son, William C. Collings, and here it is to-day in the possession of one who is justly proud of owning such a relic and having fixed it into a cap gun, makes frequent use of it.

Zebulon Collings built a fine brick house near the site of the fort and lived there until his death. This farm is now owned by James Ferguson.

The best logs were taken from "Long Knife's" house and used in building a loom-house for Elab Collings (grandson).

Elab Collings had a log house near the site of his grandfather's historic home where he lived; here his family were born and raised.

Sherman Collings (son of Elab) tells that when he was but a lad he would pick the bullets from his father's loom-house. These had been placed in the original home of his grandfather.

The last house of this early time was one hundred yards west from the monument.

Dr. John Richie and Sichey Collings were the first people married in Scott County. Their oldest child was born October 12, 1812, six weeks after the massacre.

While the Indians were on their ill-fated trip at Pigeon Roost, they took Ginsey McCoy, a neice of Mrs. Jeremiah Payne's. Some fifteen or sixteen years afterwards a white man saw a white child with a band of Indians at their camp on the Kankakee River. He asked them where they got the child. They said, "On the Pigeon Roost raid." He sent word to the people of Scott County, and immediately a militia under the command of Captain Christian Bridgewater started (for they well knew who the child was). Among the number was William Cravens (father of Nelson and William) who carried a rifle gun and had a saddle bag filled with biscuits. The trip was unsuccessful, for

26

the Indians were gone. The company was on the search for two weeks. This little girl was three years old at the time of her capture. After many years, her uncle, Isaac McCoy and wife (missionaries among the Indians) were traveling through Kansas, Arkansas and Missouri. While on this mission they found the lost child. Through all the life she had remembered her name. They found her a pretty woman with light hair and blue eyes but she had become an Indian in nature. When grown she had married an Indian chief and raised a family. Her uncle brought her back to see her relatives in Indiana but she was not content and remained but a short time. Back among her tribe and with her children she died.

This story seems more of a romance than truth but it comes to me through the Paynes, and we might say that it is authentical.

COLLINGS' GENEALOGY.

A. William E. Collings.
  1   Elizabeth.
  2   Zebulon.
  3   Richard.
  4   Henry.
  5   James Collings Biggs (John).
  6   Sichey Collings Richie (John).
  7   John.
      1   Zebulon (wife Elizabeth).
          Isaac Collings, Bloomington.
          Laman Collings, Hanover, Colorado.
          Minerva Howe, Underwood.
          Frank.
          Sarah Alsup.
      2   Joseph, deceased (wife Sallie).
      3   Jane Collings Rose.
          Nannie Applegate.
          Frank.
          Sadie Broda.
          Lida Broda.
          Zebulon.
          Ida.
  8   Karnes.
      1   William E.
          Michael.
          Sallie Jones.
          Louis.
      2   Zebulon.
          (A) Amos.

27

Gran Hagland, Vienna.
Mary M.
Clyde R.
Jane E.
Ray M.
Netta L.
Earle C.

(B) Nancy Collings Murphy, deceased (husband,
    Anna Mount, Scottsburg.   [Sam.)
    Mattie Davis, Indianapolis.
    Hartwell, Indianapolis.
    Jessie Mount, Indianapolis.
    Maggie.
    Amos, Louisville.
    James, Scottsburg.
    Homer.
    Zebia.

Karnes.
First wife, Mary Jane Hoagland.
  Elizabeth Rogers.
  Rachael.
Second wife, Cynthia Highland.
  Hezekiah.
Third wife, Elizabeth Harden.
  William E.
  Gemina.
  Phebe Montgomery.
  Betsey Louis.
  John.
  Eva Hall.
  Floyd.

4 Elab (wife, Lieuvina).
  1 William C. (wife, Anna).
    Edgar, Jeffersonville.
    Anna ——— Underwood.
    Pearl Worman, Jeffersonville.
    Wilbur.
    Elmer.
    Elsie.
    Homer.
  2 Elab S. (wife, Metta).
    Jane Eunice.
    Alice May.
  3 George R. (wife, Anna E.).
    Ida C.
    Bessie Eunice.
  4 Jane Gray, (widow).

                Belle.
                Joe.
                Lou Johnson.
                Sallie Finley.
                Emma Collings.
                William.
                Hayes.
        5   Kate Worman.
                Ed Worman.
                Nora Reed.
                Ella.
                Friedley.
                Logan.
                Claude.
        6   Margaret Wroth.
                First husband, Henthorn.
                James.
                William.
                John.
                Second husband, Martin Wroth.
                Addie Ricesinger.
                Martin.
                Caroline.
                Bertha.
        7   Phebe Rose.
                Daniel Boone.
                Gran Richie.
                Lola.
                Ida.
                Amos.
                Zebulon.
                Sherman.
        8   Ida Bennett.
                Edith.
                Leslie.
                Agnes.

CRAVEN'S GENEALOGY

William Cravens.
    First wife, Nellie Bridgewater.
        1   John Nelson, Scottsburg.
                Mary Frances Smith.
                Josephine Bridgewater.
                Margaret Adelaide Montgomery.
                Cordelia Smith.
                Katherine Ellen Robins.

2 William, Scottsburg.
    Elmira Samples.
    Lania Garrett.
    Minerva Storm.
    Alfred Cravens.
    Kate McClane.
    Flora Gardner.
3 Vincent, Madison.
    Eva Ramsey.
    Lincoln Cravens.
    Carrie Cravens.
Second wife, Rachael Fount.
    1 Mary Cravens Wiley.
        Walter.

PAYNE'S GENEALOGY.

Jeremiah Payne, wife Sarah McCoy.
    1 Louis, wife Susana Dawalt.
        1 William.
        2 Henry.
            1 William.
            2 Dora.
            3 Jordan.
            4 Emma.
            5 Ora.
            6 Bryan.
            7 Lenard.
        3 Jeremiah.
        4 Catherine.
        5 Daniel.
        6 Sarah.
        7 James.
        8 John.
    2 William, wife, Elizabeth Dewalt.
        1 Sarah.
        2 James.
        3 Mary Ann.
        4 Linia.
        5 Richard.
        6 Henry.
        7 Martha.
        8 Harriett.
    3 Simon.
        Had one daughter who married Nathan Mendenhall.
    4 Priscilla, married Frederic Leatherman.
        1 Margaret.

30

2 Sarah.
3 Elizabeth.
4 Mary, married Peter Cauble.
   1 Albert.
   2 Luella, married Sam Stover, had six children.
   3 Docia.
   4 George.
   5 Etta.
   6 Belle.
   7 Adda.
5 Priscilla, married Albert Overman.
   1 Clella, married Samuel Smead.
      1 Gladys.
      2 Daisy.
      3 Etta.
      4 Flora.
      5 One died in infancy.
6 Christinia, married George McMillen.
   1 Elbert.
   2 Gertrude.
   3 Rolla.
   Two died in infancy. The three oldest died
      in infancy of consumption.
5 Elizabeth, married John Whirl.
   1 Sarah.
   2 Rachel.
6 Indiana, married William Myers.
7 James, married Sophia Blades.
   1 Calvin, married Lucy Howells.
      1 Harriet.
      2 Amanda.
      3 Leander.
      4 Bina.
      5 John.
   2 Isaac.
   3 Eli.
   4 Sarah.
   5 Jacob.
   Two died when young.
8 Sarah, married Asbury Garriott.
   1 Louisa.
   2 William.
   3 James, married Sally Long.
      1 Minnie, married Harry Fulmer.
         a. Ruth.
         b. Arthur.
         c. Wade. d. Harry.

  2 Nolia, married Daniel Still, had one child.
  3 Wade, married Kate Rush.
    a. Ruth.
  4 Esther.
  5 Margaret.
  6 Charles.
  7 John.
  8 Lenard.
  9 Agnes.
 4 Sarah.
 5 Jacob.
 6 Elizabeth.
 7 Jeremiah.
9 Mary, married Jacob Day.
 1 Wesley.
 2 Elvira.
 3 Jacob.
 4 Ozena.
10 Christinia, never married.

MAP OF SETTLEMENT.

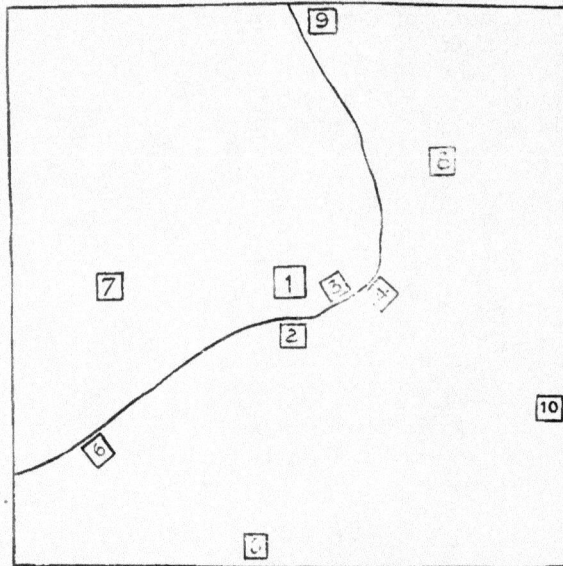

1, Monument; 2, Wm. C. Collings' home; 3, Henry Collings' home; 4, Richard Collings' home; 5, Zebulon Collings' home, where fort was; 6, Dr. Richie's home; 7, John Biggs' home; 8, Coffman's home; 9, Jeremiah Payne's home; 10, Silver Creek Fort.

John Nelson Cravens, one of Scott County's best men, is distantly related to one branch of a family that became victims during the terrible massacre. His father was William Cravens, a native of Kentucky, who came to Indiana and settled near Vienna in 1822. His mother was Nellie Bridgewater, a sister to Mrs. Elias Payne, Mrs. Isaac Coffman and Mrs. Dan Johnson.

JOHN NELSON CRAVENS.

His stepmother was Rachael Yount, the child who was born the night of the massacre in the fort at Silver Creek.

John Nelson was born July 8, 1832, in the little village of Vienna, a few miles from the sad scene of action and nineteen years after the massacre. It was a topic much talked of but little thought of as now. When growing into manhood the life

33

of the farmer was his, and Margaret Curry, a woman from Ireland shared the pleasures and trials of his home. Three children came to gladden the hearth stone—all now grown and mothers in their own homes: Mary Frances Smith, Vienna; Josephine Bridgewater; Margaret Adelaide Montgomery.

Mr. Cravens' second wife was Nancy Jane Law. The children of this union were Cordelia Smith and Kathrina Ellen Robins.

During the sixties Mr. Cravens was enlisted in the service of his country but was crippled while on the field and returned home within a year. To-day "Uncle Nelson" is one of the best known and highly respected farmers of Scott County. And it is with a tinge of regret that he recalls stories of the sad massacre. His one regret is that he does not remember and know more.

A BRIEF REVIEW OF SCOTT COUNTY HISTORY.

In 1805 the first settlements were made in what is now known as Scott County. These early inhabitants settled near Nabb and John Kimberlin was the first settler. The crudeness of the living and the hardships of these people is almost imaginable. Then occurred in 1812 the terrible, historic massacre that greatly changed the atmosphere of living.

In 1820 a new county was formed from parts of Jennings, Jefferson, Clark and Washington Counties, that was known as Scott County. It was named in honor of General Charles Scott, a hero of the Revolution, who afterwards became governor of Kentucky. This county is very irregular in shape and contains 213 square miles. The county seat was at Lexington for fifty-three years, but July 4, 1873, the corner stone for a new court house was laid at Scottsburg and the municiple headquarters were changed to a more central place.

In 1884 Scottsburg was incorporated. To-day it is a thriving little town of about fifteen hundred, with four churches, a number of lodges and a good telephone system.

For many years Scott County was considered almost as a "black sheep." Seemingly they could not find what their talent was—now along agricultural lines they are sure alive. The following will show what has been done in recent years:

The first tomato cannery in this part of the State was established at Underwood, in Clark County, immediately across the south line of Scott County, 1892. Followed by one at Vienna, Scott County in 1893. Then one at Lexington in 1895, and one at Scottsburg, the county seat, 1899, and one at Austin in 1901. Ox Valley and Leota followed in 1903. The second one in Austin will be completed and ready for the crop of tomatoes in 1904. Scott County is now noted for the growing and packing of a superior quality of red ripe tomatoes. The tomatoes grown in Scott County are noted for being solid of meat, few of seeds, rich red color and of unexcelled flavor.

The tomato growers of this county will during the tomato season of 1904 deliver to eleven different tomato canneries, seven of this number being within her own borders, and more being promoted. There will be more than 4,000 acres planted tomatoes in this county in 1904. Scottsburg, the county seat, is the central shipping point for these factories, the most prosperous one being located there, and owned and operated by Mr. Preston and John W. Rider, known as The Scottsburg Canning Company. Mr. Preston Rider resides at Columbus, Indiana, where he owns and operates a large canning and can plant. Mr. J. W. Rider, being the active member of the Scottsburg Canning Company, with Mr. Logan Hooker as superintendent. This plant has grown from 1899, packing only a few cases of tomatoes, until at the present time it has a floor space of 22,858 square feet. And now packing tomatoes, lye hominy, string beans, apples, pumpkins and tomato pulp. Their goods are all packed under their well known brand, "Royal Gem" and Ye Olden Times and Old Mammy Brands Lye Hominy, which stand at the head of the list in the market.

Besides this, wheat is quite a success. The various mills show the value of the timber. There are several towns in the county. Among the early inhabitants we find the names of those distantly related to the Collings and others of the massacre.

AN OLD HISTORIC TREE.

There is standing on a hillside
  Near Scott County's boundary line,
A large tree of wondrous measure,
  Standing through long years of time.

All have heard its early history,
  Eighty years it now has been
Since upon our pioneer settlers
  Came twelve Shawnee Indian men.

Many a time our state had suffered
  From the fierce and savage fight,
But this one was the bloodiest
  Fought in early autumn light.

Twenty-two in all were numbered;
  Men and women, babe and child;

35

Mercy ne'er was shown by savage
  When his brain for blood is wild.

Then the soldiers of Clark County
  Gathered up the slaughtered dead,
Laid them sorrowfully and tender
  In this our common bed.

When soon sprang the sturdy sassafras,
  And its mission seems to be
To mark this grave of the settlers,
  That posterity may see.

Though it stood the winds of winter,
  And the storms for many years,
It is dying; as we note it
  Eyes are almost filled with tears.

Many of its boughs have fallen,
  Though the sturdy trunk stands still;
But not many years in future
  Will it stand upon the hill.

Nature's acts are always noble,
  Where's a deed more nobly done,
Than for her to plan a grave-stone
  Where the hands of man put none?

Why is not a fitting monument
  Put upon these pioneer's graves,
To the memory of our ancestors,
  To the memory of our braves?
                    Mattie Jean Wright.

36